A complete spelling programme
Year 3

raintree
Babcock ldp

Raintree is an imprint of Capstone Global Library Limited, a company incorporated in England and Wales having its registered office at 7 Pilgrim Street, London, EC4V 6LB – Registered company number: 6695582

www.raintree.co.uk
myorders@raintree.co.uk

Text © Capstone Global Library Limited 2016
The moral rights of the proprietor have been asserted.

All rights reserved. No part of this publication may be reproduced in any form or by any means (including photocopying or storing it in any medium by electronic means and whether or not transiently or incidentally to some other use of this publication) without the written permission of the copyright owner, except in accordance with the provisions of the Copyright, Designs and Patents Act 1988 or under the terms of a licence issued by the Copyright Licensing Agency, Saffron House, 6–10 Kirby Street, London EC1N 8TS (www.cla.co.uk). Applications for the copyright owner's written permission should be addressed to the publisher.

Devised and written by Rebecca Cosgrave, Jenny Core, Joy Simpson and Angela Sykes of the Babcock LDP Primary English Team.
Edited by Clare Lewis
Designed by Richard Parker and HL Studios
Picture research by Eric Gohl
Production by Helen McCreath
Originated by Capstone Global Library Ltd
Printed in China

ISBN 978 1 4747 0999 6
19 18 17
10 9 8 7 6 5

Pack
ISBN 978 1 4747 0981 1
19 18 17
10 9 8 7 6 5

British Library Cataloguing in Publication Data
A full catalogue record for this book is available from the British Library.

Acknowledgements
National Curriculum extract p. 11 © Crown copyright information licensed under the Open Government Licence v3.0.

All images provided by Shutterstock

Every effort has been made to contact copyright holders of material reproduced in this book. Any omissions will be rectified in subsequent printings if notice is given to the publisher.

All the Internet addresses (URLs) given in this book were valid at the time of going to press. However, due to the dynamic nature of the Internet, some addresses may have changed, or sites may have changed or ceased to exist since publication. While the author and publisher regret any inconvenience this may cause readers, no responsibility for any such changes can be accepted by either the author or the publisher.

Contents

Introduction	4
What is the *No Nonsense Spelling* Programme?	4
Assessment	6
Complementary resources	7
Learning spellings	9
Year 3 National Curriculum requirements	12
Year 3 Lesson plans	13
Year 3 Term 1 overview	13
Block 1 – autumn first half term	15
Block 2 – autumn second half term	21
Year 3 Term 2 overview	26
Block 3 – spring first half term	28
Block 4 – spring second half term	33
Year 3 Term 3 overview	37
Block 5 – summer first half term	39
Block 6 – summer second half term	45
Statutory word list for Years 3 and 4	49
Year 3 Supporting Resources	50

Introduction

What is the *No Nonsense Spelling* Programme?

The *No Nonsense Spelling* Programme was devised to offer teachers a comprehensive yet accessible progression in the teaching of spelling. Guidance, rather than prescription, is provided on how to teach the strategies, knowledge and skills pupils need to learn.

The focus of the programme is on the *teaching* of spelling, which embraces knowledge of spelling conventions – patterns and rules; but integral to the teaching is the opportunity to promote the *learning* of spellings, including statutory words, common exceptions and personal spellings.

The programme

- delivers a manageable tool for meeting the requirements of the 2014 National Curriculum
- has a clear progression through blocks of teaching units across the year
- comprehensively explains how to teach spelling effectively.

How *No Nonsense Spelling* is organised

The programme consists of the following elements:

- The requirements of the National Curriculum, which have been organised into strands and then broken down into termly overviews. The overall pathway can be found on the USB stick.
- Termly overviews that have been mapped across weeks as half termly plans. These follow a model of five spelling sessions across two weeks, except in Year 2 where sessions are daily.
- Daily lesson plans for each session, with Supporting Resources, including word lists and guidance on conventions.

The lesson plans

The lessons themselves then follow the structure below:

Lesson	Reference to year group, block of lessons and lesson number in sequence
Lesson type	Revise/Teach/Learn/Practise/Apply/Assess
Lesson focus	The particular spelling focus for the day
Resources needed	A list of the resources that will be needed. These might be documents that are photocopied or printed in advance so that flashcards can be prepared, or presentations to display the task/activity on a whiteboard. The resources are featured at the end of each book for reference. Editable versions are available on the USB stick, which can be copied and pasted into your own documents and edited.
Teaching activity	Key teaching points, sometimes including extra notes and tips for the teacher

Each lesson is approximately 10 to15 minutes long, but lesson plans are flexible so that the teaching can reflect the extra time needed on a teaching point if required. The Supporting Resources at the back of each book can be used as appropriate to adjust the pace and focus of the lesson. Each lesson clearly signposts when additional resources from the Programme can be used.

Supporting Resources

The Supporting Resources include picture and word lists, which can be photocopied and made into flashcards or used in classroom displays, and pictures. They also include games and quizzes. The Resources are featured at the end of each book for reference and as editable Word documents on the USB stick, which can be copied and pasted to be used on classroom whiteboards and in other documents.

Teaching sequence

The programme has been written broadly following a teaching sequence for spelling, whereby each new concept is taught, practised and then applied and assessed. Frequently there is also a 'Revise' session before the teaching session. A typical teaching sequence is as follows:

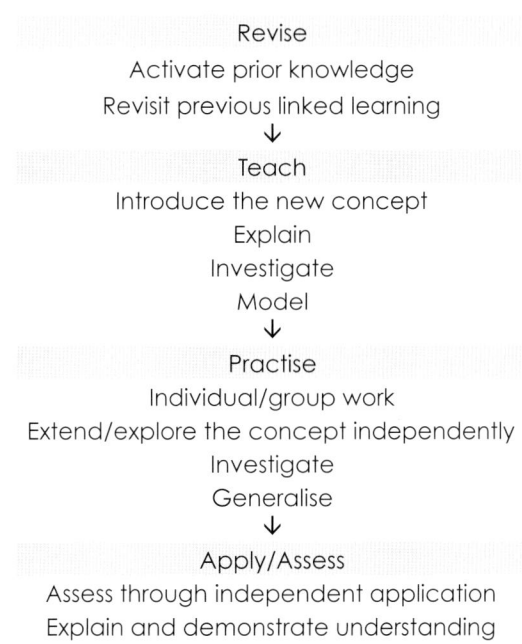

Within the lessons, the particular focus is identified, followed by suggested teaching strategies.

By integrating activities for handwriting, the benefit of making a spelling activity kinaesthetic is secured. The pupil acquires the physical memory of the spelling pattern as well as the visual. Integral to the process is the scope to encourage pupils to learn spellings. The value of a school policy and possible approaches are explored further on page 9, 'Learning spellings'.

You will find the following referred to in the lessons:
Modelling: An activity is described, and it is anticipated that the action expected of pupils is modelled to them first.
Spelling partners: Pupils are asked to work in pairs, often to 'test' each other. They will be asked to work with their spelling partner from time to time.

Assessment

Pupils' learning is assessed throughout the programme. The 'Apply' part of the sequence regularly includes assessment activities to identify if pupils have learnt the key concept taught. These activities include:

- Testing – by teacher and peers
- Dictation
- Explaining
- Independent application in writing
- Frequent learning and testing of statutory and personal words.

Error Analysis

Error Analysis can be used to assess what strategies pupils are using in their day-to-day writing. It can also help identify where to put emphasis in the programme – for the whole class, groups or individuals. Error Analysis can also be repeated to assess progress over a longer period of time.

A template for a suggested grid for Error Analysis can be found in the Supporting Resources.

How to complete an Error Analysis:

1. Choose one piece of independent writing from each pupil.
2. Identify all the spelling errors and record them on the grid. Decide what you think is the main source of the error and record the word in the corresponding column. It is a good idea to record the word as the pupil has spelt it.
3. Identify any patterns. Quite quickly you will be able to see which aspect of spelling needs to be addressed.

The headings included on the grid are

- Common exception words
- GPCs (grapheme–phoneme correspondences) including rarer GPCs and vowel digraphs
- Homophones
- Prefixes and suffixes
- Word endings
- Other.

These headings correspond to key strands within the National Curriculum. These could be changed or further areas added if needed.

Year					
Common exception words	GPC (includes rare GPCs and vowel digraphs)	Homophones	Prefixes and suffixes	Word endings	Others
firend whent	perants fir clouser (closer) flow (flew) amzing nealy eaven	their (there) x2.	phond horrerfied		orgorment argement

Complementary resources

To support the teaching, additional resources are recommended and referred to throughout the programme.

Spelling journals	Developing the use of spelling journals can support both teachers and pupils in many ways. They enable • pupils to take responsibility for their spelling learning • pupils to refer back to previous learning • teachers to see how pupils are tackling tricky bits of spelling • teachers and pupils to discuss spelling with parents and carers Spelling journals can take many forms and are much more than just a word book. Spelling journals can be used for  • practising strategies • learning words • recording rules/conventions/generalisations as an aide-memoire • word lists of really tricky words (spelling enemies) • 'Having a go' at the point of writing • ongoing record of statutory words learnt 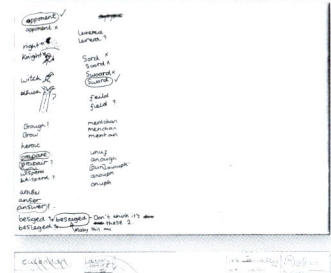 • investigations • recording spelling targets or goals • spelling tests. In the programme, there is flexibility for journals to be set up in a variety of ways. Below are a few recommendations: 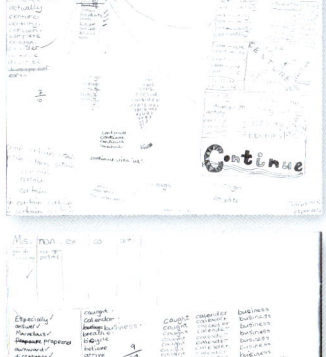 • Make sure that the journal can be used flexibly. A blank exercise book gives much more scope for pupils to try out ideas and organise their learning than a heavily structured format. • Model different ways of using the journal. A class spelling journal or examples from different pupils could be used to do this.  • Give time for pupils to use their journals and to review them. • Do the majority of spelling work in the journal.

Have a go sheets	These are a key component of Strategies at the point of writing. They are introduced in the Year 2 programme and then revisited in Years 3, 4, 5 and 6. Schools need to decide how Have a go will form part of their spelling policy, together with the use of spelling journals and establishing routines for attempting unknown spellings. A Have a go sheet template is provided in the Supporting Resources. Have a go sheets can take several different forms, for example: • a large sheet of paper on a table that pupils write on when they need to • sheets stuck in all pupils' books that fold out when pupils are writing • a book placed on the table open at a clean sheet for pupils to use • a page in pupils' spelling journals. **Note:** it is important that teachers have an enlarged version of a Have a go sheet displayed for modelling when writing in any curriculum area and at any time in the school day. Introducing Have a Go: 1. Model writing a sentence and being unsure about how to spell a word. Talk about the tricky part in the word and some of the choices you might have for that part. You could refer to a GPC chart to find the choices if appropriate. 2. Model writing the word with two or three choices on your own enlarged version of a Have a go sheet and then model choosing the one that you think looks right and using it in your sentence. It is important that pupils learn to ask themselves the question 'Does it look right?' or 'Have I seen it like this in a book?' to help them make their choices. 3. If you are still unsure of the spelling, put a wiggly line under it in the sentence to signal that this needs checking by the teacher, or the pupil if appropriate, during proofreading time. 4. Model continuing with writing and *not* checking the correct version of the spelling at this point. This is important so that the flow of writing is not unnecessarily slowed. 5. Make sure you model this process briefly in writing in all curriculum areas. 6. Pupils use their own Have a Go sheet (or group sheet) whenever they write and refer to GPC charts and other classroom displays as support, as well as specific strategies that have been taught for using at the point of writing. 7. Remind them never to make more than three attempts at a word. Misspelt words will need to be corrected in line with your school's spelling and marking policy. Some of these words may be included in pupils' individual word lists for learning. To see lessons where Have a go strategies are first introduced, please refer to Year 2 Block 1 Lessons 11 and 17.
GPC (grapheme-phoneme correspondence) choices chart	The teaching of spelling complements very much the teaching of phonics. It is anticipated that the school will draw upon the GPC charts used in their phonics programme to work alongside the teaching of spelling.

Individual whiteboards	Individual whiteboards can be used in a variety of ways to support lessons including checking spelling attempts, Quickwrite and Have a go.
Working wall	It is really useful to have a small area of display space in the classroom that can reflect current teaching focuses and provide support for pupils' spelling as they write. GPC charts, reminders of common spelling patterns or conventions and tricky words to remember could be part of a working wall for spelling.

Learning spellings

A school policy can help inform

- the strategies for learning spellings that are being taught
- routines for learning spellings
- links with home learning.

Learning needs to happen in school and at home. There is little evidence, though, that the traditional practice of learning spellings (usually 10) at home and being tested on them (usually on a Friday) is effective. However, there is a high expectation within the new National Curriculum that pupils will learn many increasingly complex words. Within the programme, learning spellings is built into each six-week block. Within the sessions a range of strategies for learning spellings are introduced and practised. This enables pupils to choose the strategies they find most effective for learning different words.

Tips for learning spellings at home

Learning at home needs to be an extension of the practice in school. Consider

- limiting the number of words to five or less a week to ensure success and enable deeper learning
- making sure pupils and parents have access to the range of learning strategies which have been taught in school, to use in home learning
- assessing spellings in context, for example: learning spellings in a given sentence, generating sentences for each word, assessing through unseen dictated sentences
- keeping an ongoing record of words learnt and setting very high expectations of correct application in writing once a word has been learned.

The learning strategies on the next two pages are introduced incrementally throughout the programme and can then be used to support learning spellings at home.

Look, say, cover, write, check	This is probably the most common strategy used to learn spellings. **Look**: first look at the whole word carefully and if there is one part of the word that is difficult, look at that part in more detail. **Say**: say the word as you look at it, using different ways of pronouncing it if that will make it more memorable. **Cover**: cover the word. **Write**: write the word from memory, saying the word as you do so. **Check**: Have you got it right? If yes, try writing it again and again! If not, start again – look, say, cover, write, check.
Trace, copy and replicate (and then check)	This is a similar learning process to 'look, say, cover, write, check' but is about developing automaticity and muscle memory. Write the word out on a sheet of paper ensuring that it is spelt correctly and it is large enough to trace over. Trace over the word and say it at the same time. Move next to the word you have just written and write it out as you say it. Turn the page over and write the word as you say it, and then check that you have spelt it correctly. If this is easy, do the same process for two different words at the same time. Once you have written all your words this way and feel confident, miss out the tracing and copying or the tracing alone and just write the words.
Segmentation strategy	The splitting of a word into its constituent phonemes in the correct order to support spelling.
Quickwrite	Writing the words linked to the teaching focus with speed and fluency. The aim is to write as many words as possible within a time constraint. Pupils can write words provided by the teacher or generate their own examples. For example, in two minutes write as many words as possible with the /iː/ phoneme. This can be turned into a variety of competitive games including working in teams and developing relay race approaches.
Drawing around the word to show the shape	Draw around the words making a clear distinction in size where there are ascenders and descenders. Look carefully at the shape of the word and the letters in each box. Now try to write the word making sure that you get the same shape. t o t a l l y

Drawing an image around the word	This strategy is all about making a word memorable. It links to meaning in order to try to make the spelling noticeable. *Monarchy* You can't use this method as your main method of learning spellings, but it might work on those that are just a little more difficult to remember.
Words without vowels	This strategy is useful where the vowel choices are the challenge in the words. Write the words without the vowels and pupils have to choose the correct grapheme to put in the space. For example, for the word *field*: f_____ld
Pyramid words	This method of learning words forces you to think of each letter separately. p py pyr pyra pyram pyrami pyramid You can then reverse the process so that you end up with a diamond.
Other strategies	Other methods can include: - Rainbow writing. Using coloured pencils in different ways can help to make parts of words memorable. You could highlight the tricky parts of the word or write the tricky part in a different colour. You could also write each letter in a different colour, or write the word in red, then overlay in orange, yellow and so on. - Making up memorable 'silly sentences' containing the word - Saying the word in a funny way – for example, pronouncing the 'silent' letters in a word - Clapping and counting to identify the syllables in a word.

Year 3 National Curriculum requirements

Pupils should be taught to

- develop a range of personal strategies for learning new and irregular words*
- develop a range of personal strategies for spelling at the point of composition*
- develop a range of strategies for checking and proofreading spellings after writing*
- use further prefixes and suffixes and understand how to add them (English Appendix 1)
- spell further homophones
- spell words that are often misspelt (English Appendix 1)
- place the possessive apostrophe accurately in words with regular plurals (for example, *girls'*, *boys'*) and in words with irregular plurals (for example, *children's*)
- use the first two or three letters of a word to check its spelling in a dictionary
- write from memory simple sentences, dictated by the teacher, that include words and punctuation taught so far
- proofread for spelling errors.

* non-statutory

Year 3 lesson plans

Year 3 Term 1 overview

Block 1 – autumn first half term

Week 1	Lesson 1 Revise **Suffixes from Year 2: '-s', '-es', '-er', '-ed', '-ing'**	Lesson 2 Practise **Suffixes from Year 2: '-s', '-es', '-er', '-ed', '-ing'**	Lesson 3 Revise/Teach **Revise prefix 'un-'** **Teach prefix 'dis-'** (*disappoint, disagree, disobey*)
Week 2	Lesson 4 Practise/Apply **Practise prefix 'dis-'** **Apply prefix 'un-'**	Lesson 5 Revise **From Year 2: apostrophe for contraction**	
Week 3	Lesson 6 Learn **Strategies for learning words: words from statutory and personal spelling lists**	Lesson 7 Revise/Teach **Strategies at the point of writing: Have a go**	
Week 4	Lesson 8 Teach **Rarer GPCs: words with the /eɪ/ sound spelt 'ei' (*vein*), 'eigh' (*eight*), 'aigh' (*straight*) or 'ey' (*they*)**	Lesson 9 Practise **Rarer GPCs: words with the /eɪ/ sound spelt 'ei' (*vein*), 'eigh' (*eight*), 'aigh' (*straight*) or 'ey' (*they*)**	Lesson 10 Assess **Rarer GPCs: words with the /eɪ/ sound spelt 'ei' (*vein*), 'eigh' (*eight*), 'aigh' (*straight*) or 'ey' (*they*): dictation**
Week 5	Lesson 11 Learn **Strategies for learning words: words from statutory and personal spelling lists**	Lesson 12 Teach **Homophones (*brake/break, grate/great, eight/ate, weight/wait, son/sun*)**	
Week 6	Lesson 13 Practise **Homophones (*brake/break, grate/great, eight/ate, weight/wait, son/sun*)**	Lesson 14 Assess **Homophones (*brake/break, grate/great, eight/ate, weight/wait, son/sun*)**	

Block 2 – autumn second half term

Week 1	Lesson 1 Revise **Statutory words learnt last half term** **Strategies at the point of writing: Have a go**	Lesson 2 Revise **Homophones**	Lesson 3 Revise **Year 2 prefixes and suffixes**
Week 2	Lesson 4 Teach **Prefixes 'mis-' and 're-'**	Lesson 5 Practise **Prefixes 'mis-' and 're-'**	
Week 3	Lesson 6 Apply **Prefixes 'mis-' and 're-'**	Lesson 7 Learn **Strategies for learning words: words from statutory and personal spelling lists**	
Week 4	Lesson 8 Assess **Words from statutory and personal spelling lists: pair-testing**	Lesson 9 Teach **The /ɪ/ sound spelt 'y'**	Lesson 10 Practise/Apply **The /ɪ/ sound spelt 'y'**
Week 5	Lesson 11 Teach **Proofreading**	Lesson 12 Practise **Proofreading**	
Week 6	Lesson 13 Learn **Strategies for learning words: words from statutory and personal spelling lists**	Lesson 14 Teach **Words ending with the /g/ sound spelt '-gue' and the /k/ sound spelt '-que' (French in origin)**	

Block 1 – autumn first half term

Lesson	Year 3, block 1, lesson 1
Lesson type	Revise
Lesson focus	**Suffixes from Year 2: '-s', '-es', '-er', '-ed', '-ing'**
Resources needed	Supporting Resource 3.4
Teaching activity	Display a range of verbs and, as a class, add the above endings. Talk through why there needs to be spelling changes for some of the verbs. Show the chart in the Supporting Resource. Pupils record the verbs adding on endings. They check with partners that they are correct, then share as a class. **Notes:** • A short vowel sound indicates a doubling of the consonant. • Verbs ending in 'e' have the 'e' removed before adding '-ed' or '-ing'. Show what happens when you double the consonant and when you take off an 'e'. Pupils make notes about this in their spelling journals.

Lesson	Year 3, block 1, lesson 2
Lesson type	Practise
Lesson focus	**Suffixes from Year 2: '-s', '-es', '-er', '-ed', '-ing'**
Resources needed	Supporting Resources 3.5 (poem)
Teaching activity	Check that pupils can recall examples of suffixes from the previous lesson. Use the poem from the Supporting Resource and ask pupils to rewrite it as a poem about yesterday. Make up a poem about the class, and get pupils to add their own lines. Emphasise the correct spelling of the verbs.

Lesson	Year 3, block 1, lesson 3
Lesson type	Revise/Teach
Lesson focus	**Revise prefix 'un-'** **Teach prefix 'dis-' (*disappoint, disagree, disobey*)**
Resources needed	Supporting Resource 3.6 (prefix word cards)
Teaching activity	Discuss the term 'prefix'. Put two columns on your board – one headed 'un-' and one headed 'dis-'. Take a pile of word cards from the resource and sort them into the correct side of the chart, discussing how the prefix affects the meaning of the word. Get pupils to practise handwriting 'un-' and 'dis-'. Call out some more of the words and pupils write them down three times with the correct prefix, focusing on handwriting.

Block 1 – autumn first half term

Lesson	Year 3, block 1, lesson 4
Lesson type	Practise/Apply
Lesson focus	**Practise 'dis-'** **Apply prefix 'un-'**
Resources needed	Spelling journals
Teaching activity	Ask pupils to tell their partners and then you what a prefix is. They should suggest some that they know. Write a word on the whiteboard and ask pupils to write the opposite down using a prefix. Dictate a sentence or two using the words. **Examples:** *He disliked this unkind boy.* *The king was displeased.* *He was disappointed because it was raining.*

Lesson	Year 3, block 1, lesson 5
Lesson type	Revise
Lesson focus	**From Year 2: Apostrophe for contraction**
Resources needed	Supporting Resource 3.7 (apostrophe phrase cards)
Teaching activity	Display the following sentences. Ask pupils to tell you what an apostrophe is and to find some in these sentences: *'Don't stay up too late,' shouted Mum.* *I didn't get any biscuits so you can't dunk them in your tea.* Where are they used and why? Read out or display some phrases from the resource. Pupils contract them and write the contractions in their journals. They mark each other's work in pairs and identify those that were not correct. Spend some time practising the words with Quickwrite. If pupils are not secure with these apostrophes for contractions, put in extra sessions for further practice.

Block 1 – autumn first half term

Lesson	Year 3, block 1, lesson 6
Lesson type	Learn
Lesson focus	**Strategies for learning words: words from statutory and personal lists**
Resources needed	Statutory word list for Years 3 and 4 (page 49)
Teaching activity	Introduce a learning strategy to pupils such as Pyramids. Pupils identify the tricky part of the word in up to five statutory words and try writing that bit as many times as possible in 30 seconds. Then do as below for each word: s s h s h o s h o u s h o u l s h o u l d Or do this in reverse. Practise this on the five words from the statutory list. Send words home for further practice. Encourage pupils to use learning strategies that work best for them.

Lesson	Year 3, block 1, lesson 7
Lesson type	Revise/ Teach
Lesson focus	**Strategies at the point of writing: Have a go**
Resources needed	Supporting Resources 3.2 (Have a go template) and 3.3 (GPC chart)
Teaching activity	Reintroduce the use of Have a go sheets (see Introduction page 8). Make sure pupils have access to and understand how to use a GPC chart to support spelling choices at the point of writing.

Block 1 – autumn first half term

Lesson	Year 3, block 1, lesson 8
Lesson type	Teach
Lesson focus	**Rarer GPCs: words with the** /eɪ/ **sound spelt 'ei' (***vein***), 'eigh' (***eight***), 'aigh' (***straight***) or 'ey' (***they***)**
Resources needed	Supporting Resource 3.8 (/eɪ/ sound list)
Teaching activity	Ask pupils to name as many ways as possible that they know of to spell the /eɪ/ sound. Add some words such as *they, eight, eighty, eighteen, straight, vein*. Pupils record them in a chart according to the grapheme for /eɪ/. Which spellings do you find where? This can be differentiated so that some pupils only work with three spellings of /eɪ/, for example 'ai', 'ay' and 'a-e'

Lesson	Year 3, block 1, lesson 9
Lesson type	Practise
Lesson focus	**Rarer GPCs: words with the** /eɪ/ **sound spelt 'ei' (***vein***), 'eigh' (***eight***), 'aigh' (***straight***) or 'ey' (***they***)**
Resources needed	Supporting Resources 3.8 (/eɪ/ sound and homophones list) and 3.9 (/eɪ/ pictures)
Teaching activity	Play Countdown in pairs. Pupils time each other to read as many of the /eɪ/ sound words as they can from the list. Next, show the pictures. Pupils work out the words. They are: *rain, snake, brake, eight, sleigh, spade, tail, tray, shake, play, paint, grey* Model writing a word down and making a choice about the /eɪ/ grapheme and whether it looks right. Pupils sound out the words and write them down.

Block 1 – autumn first half term

Lesson	Year 3, block 1, lesson 10
Lesson type	Assess
Lesson focus	Rarer GPCs: words with the /eɪ/ sound spelt 'ei' (*vein*), 'eigh' (*eight*), 'ey' (*they*): dictation
Resources needed	Spelling journals
Teaching activity	Get pupils to practise handwriting the words *they, day, made* and *baby*. Dictate the following sentences and then check handwriting and spellings: They went away for the day. The sale was on Monday. We weighed the eight carrots and cooked them. It is a grey day and Agent Snail is surveying the sleigh.

Lesson	Year 3, block 1, lesson 11
Lesson type	Learn
Lesson focus	Strategies for learning words: words from statutory and personal spelling lists
Resources needed	Statutory word list for Years 3 and 4 (page 49), personal spelling lists
Teaching activity	Go over the words from statutory list learnt in lesson 6 and see if spellings have been remembered. Introduce another spelling strategy such as Trace, copy and replicate (see page 10). Provide pupils with a piece of paper folded into three columns, with chosen statutory words written in a list in the first column. Pupils add their personal words to the list in the first column, making sure they are spelt correctly. Instruct pupils to trace over the words, first time saying them out loud as they do so. Next, they write the words in the second column, trying to keep the same rhythm and saying them out loud again. They then fold the paper over and write the words from memory. Do this for the rest of the words. Tell pupils to practise these words at home by putting them into sentences and writing them out.

Block 1 – autumn first half term

Lesson	Year 3, block 1, lesson 12
Lesson type	Teach
Lesson focus	**Homophones (*brake/break, grate/great, eight/ate, weight/wait, son/sun*)**
Resources needed	Supporting Resource 3.8 (/eɪ/ sound and homophones list)
Teaching activity	Explain that a homophone is a word that sounds the same but is spelt differently and means something different. 'Homo' means 'same' and 'phone' means 'sound'. Show some homophones and pupils orally compose sentences to use them in context. Use homophones that are unfamiliar to the class, for example: *where/wear* as well as *there/their/they're, break/brake, son/sun* and *eight/ate*. Teach the difference in meaning and link to something that might make them memorable. **Notes:** *There* means 'over there' like 'over here'. *Their* means it belongs to someone. *They're* is a contraction for 'they are'.

Lesson	Year 3, block 1, lesson 13
Lesson type	Practise
Lesson focus	**Homophones (*brake/break, grate/great, eight/ate, weight/wait, son/sun*)**
Resources needed	Supporting Resource 3.10 (homophone sentences)
Teaching activity	Display the sentences with missing words from the Supporting Resource. Pupils choose the correct homophone to go in them. (Answers: there, their, They're, sun, son, eight, ate, wear, Where, break, brake) For homework, pupils could take the homophones home and create their own sentences.

Lesson	Year 3, block 1, lesson 14
Lesson type	Assess
Lesson focus	**Homophones (*brake/break, grate/great, eight/ate, weight/wait, son/sun*)**
Resources needed	Supporting Resource 3.11 (/eɪ/ homophone pictures)
Teaching activity	Hand out sheets with the images on. Ask pupils to write down the correct homophone under each image. (Answers: there, where, break, sun, son, wear, eight, brake) In pairs, pupils proofread their own writing to see if the correct version of homophones studied is used.

Block 2 – autumn second half term

Lesson	Year 3, block 2, lesson 1
Lesson type	Revise
Lesson focus	**Statutory words learnt last half term** **Strategies at the point of writing: Have a go**
Resources needed	Spelling journals
Teaching activity	Give a spelling test for the statutory words learnt last half-term. Get pupils to peer mark the tests. Spend time learning the words that were not correct. Strategies to use as taught in previous sessions are: • Pyramid words • Trace, copy and replicate Remind pupils of Have a go strategies using GPC charts and other strategies to support them as they are writing. Continue to model these in all writing.

Lesson	Year 3, block 2, lesson 2
Lesson type	Revise
Lesson focus	**Homophones**
Resources needed	Spelling journals or individual whiteboards
Teaching activity	Ask pupils to come up to the board in pairs. Show them a pair of homophones and ask them to represent the words through drawing. The rest of the class should write the words on their whiteboards or in their spelling journals when they know what they are. Check for accuracy of spelling. Identify those that pupils are not getting correct and reteach them.

Lesson	Year 3, block 2, lesson 3
Lesson type	Revise
Lesson focus	**Year 2 prefixes and suffixes**
Resources needed	Supporting Resource 3.12 (Year 2 prefix and suffix matrices)
Teaching activity	Put pupils in pairs. Using matrices from Year 2, pupils read out a word they have created and their partner writes it down. They check spelling and then change over. Pupils identify those that they need to work on more and take them home to learn.

Block 2 – autumn second half term

Lesson	Year 3, block 2, lesson 4
Lesson type	Teach
Lesson focus	**Prefixes 'mis-' and 're-'**
Resources needed	Supporting Resource 3.13 ('mis-' and 're-' root words)
Teaching activity	Show pupils the chart of words in the Supporting Resource. Ask them to create words with 'mis-' and 're-'. What do they think 'mis-' and 're-' might mean? In pairs, pupils take cards with the root words and add 'mis' or 're'. They write them down in their spelling journals.

Lesson	Year 3, block 2, lesson 5
Lesson type	Practise
Lesson focus	**Prefixes 'mis-' and 're-'**
Resources needed	Spelling journals
Teaching activity	Refer pupils to the words they created in the last lesson. Ask them to use the words in sentences. They should write the sentences with a partner. Over the week collect words with the prefixes 'mis-' and 're-' and record them on the Working wall (see page 9).

Lesson	Year 3, block 2, lesson 6
Lesson type	Apply
Lesson focus	**Prefixes 'mis-' and 're-'**
Resources needed	Working wall
Teaching activity	Show pupils the following sentences. Ask them where they could add the prefixes 'mis-' or 're-' to make them mean the opposite. *The boy behaved as he played his video.* *He heard what his teacher had said.* Get pupils to choose three or four words that they don't know from the previous two lessons and learn them. Over the week collect words with the prefixes 'mis-' and 're-' and record them on the working wall (see page 9).

Block 2 – autumn second half term

Lesson	Year 3, block 2, lesson 7
Lesson type	Learn
Lesson focus	**Strategies for learning words: words from statutory and personal spelling lists**
Resources needed	Statutory word list for Years 3 and 4 (page 49)
Teaching activity	Revise the strategy Look, say, cover, write, check. If pupils have been through the Year 2 programme, they will be quite familiar with it. If not, use the session to show pupils how to do it. Introduce five new words from the statutory list and the individual word lists that pupils have. Ask pupils to use Look, say, cover, write, check to learn them. Pupils can take their words home to continue learning them.

Lesson	Year 3, block 2, lesson 8
Lesson type	Assess
Lesson focus	**Words from statutory and personal spelling lists: pair testing**
Resources needed	Statutory word list for Years 3 and 4 (page 49)
Teaching activity	Ask pupils to test each other in pairs. They should use the word lists they learnt yesterday. Any words that are not learnt should be carried over to an extra session the next day.

Lesson	Year 3, block 2, lesson 9
Lesson type	Teach
Lesson focus	**The /ɪ/ sound spelt 'y'**
Resources needed	Supporting Resource 3.14 ('y' pictures)
Teaching activity	Show the images from the Supporting Resource. Identify the words as a class and write them up. (Answers: gym, cygnet, myth, pyramid, mystery, Egypt) Ask pupils to sound out the word and write it on a piece of paper so that they can read it. What do they notice about all the words? Remove the words and then say what each image is and pupils write the word in their journals.

Block 2 – autumn second half term

Lesson	Year 3, block 2, lesson 10
Lesson type	Practise/Apply
Lesson focus	**The /ɪ/ sound spelt 'y'**
Resources needed	Supporting Resource 3.14 ('y' pictures)
Teaching activity	Pupils take it in turns to create a sentence for a partner based on one of the images and get them to write it. They check the spelling. They do this for at least five words.

Lesson	Year 3, block 2, lesson 11
Lesson type	Teach
Lesson focus	**Proofreading**
Resources needed	Examples of pupils' own writing
Teaching activity	Write a range of sentences up on the board that have spelling and punctuation errors from pupils' books. Ask pupils to find the errors and write them out correctly.

Lesson	Year 3, block 2, lesson 12
Lesson type	Practise
Lesson focus	**Proofreading**
Resources needed	Examples of pupils' own writing
Teaching activity	Put a star by sentences in pupils' writing with spelling and punctuation errors. Pupils go back and correct them. Get pupils to practise misspelt words in their spelling journals using one of the strategies that they have for learning spellings.

Block 2 – autumn second half term

Lesson	Year 3, block 2, lesson 13
Lesson type	Learn
Lesson focus	**Strategies for learning words: statutory and personal spelling lists**
Resources needed	Statutory word list for Years 3 and 4 (page 49), spelling journals
Teaching activity	Choose three words from their lists for each child to learn. Show pupils how to identify the tricky parts and draw around the words to show the shape of the words. If pupils followed the Year 2 programme, they will be familiar with this strategy. Ask pupils to tell a partner what they notice about the shape and how it looks. The partner should read out the words and write them down thinking about the shape.

Lesson	Year 3, block 2, lesson 14
Lesson type	Teach
Lesson focus	**Words ending in the /g/ sound spelt '-gue' and the /k/ sound spelt 'que' (French in origin)**
Resources needed	Spelling journals
Teaching activity	Share the following words on the board: *fatigue* *catalogue* What do pupils notice about the /g/ sound? Divide the polysyllabic words into syllables and draw a box for each syllable on the board. Syllabify the words and write each syllable in the boxes. Which syllables are tricky? How will pupils remember these? Repeat with *antique* and *unique*. Ask pupils to Quickwrite one word of each pattern for one minute.

Year 3 Term 2 overview

Block 3 – spring first half term

Week 1	Lesson 1 Revise/Teach **From Year 2: suffixes '-ness' and '-ful' following a consonant**	Lesson 2 Practise/Apply **From Year 2: suffixes '-ness' and '-ful' following a consonant**	
Week 2	Lesson 3 Teach **Prefixes 'sub-' and 'tele-'**	Lesson 4 Practise **Prefixes 'sub-' and 'tele-'**	Lesson 5 Apply **Prefixes 'sub-' and 'tele-'**
Week 3	Lesson 6 Practise **From Year 2: apostrophe for contraction**	Lesson 7 Learn **Strategies for learning words: words from statutory and personal spelling lists**	
Week 4	Lesson 8 Apply **Words from statutory and personal spelling lists: pair testing**	Lesson 9 Teach **Words with the /ʃ/ sound spelt 'ch' (mostly French in origin) as well as 's', 'ss(ion/ure)'**	Lesson 10 Practise **Words with the /ʃ/ sound spelt 'ch' (mostly French in origin) as well as 's', 'ss(ion/ure)'**
Week 5	Lesson 11 Apply **Words with the /ʃ/ sound spelt 'ch' (mostly French in origin) as well as 's', 'ss(ion/ure)': dictation**	Lesson 12 Learn **Strategies for learning words: words from statutory and personal spelling lists**	
Week 6	Lesson 13 Revise/Teach **Revise suffixes '-ness' and '-ful'** **Teach suffixes '-less' and '-ly'**	Lesson 14 Practise **Suffixes '-less', '-ness', '-ful' and '-ly'**	Lesson 15 Assess **Suffixes '-less', '-ness', '-ful' and '-ly': spelling test**

Block 4 – spring second half term

Week 1	Lesson 1 Practise/Revise **Strategies at the point of writing: Have a go** **Elements from the previous half term that require practice**	Lesson 2 Practise/Revise **Strategies at the point of writing: Have a go** **Elements from the previous half term that require practice**	Lesson 3 Practise/Revise **Strategies at the point of writing: Have a go** **Elements from the previous half term that require practice**
Week 2	Lesson 4 Teach **Prefixes 'super-' and 'auto-'**	Lesson 5 Practise **Prefixes 'super-' and 'auto-'**	
Week 3	Lesson 6 Apply **Prefixes 'super-' and 'auto-'**	Lesson 7 Learn **Strategies for learning words: words from statutory and personal spelling lists**	Lesson 8 Assess **Words from statutory and personal spelling lists: pair testing**
Week 4	Lesson 9 Teach **Strategies at the point of writing: homophones**	Lesson 10 Practise **Strategies at the point of writing: homophones**	
Week 5	Lesson 11 Apply **Homophones**	Lesson 12 Revise **Proofreading**	Lesson 13 Apply **Proofreading**
Week 6	Lesson 14 Learn **Strategies for learning words: words from statutory and personal spelling lists**	Lesson 15 Teach/Apply **Words with the /k/ sound spelt 'ch' (Greek in origin)**	

Block 3 – spring first half term

Lesson	Year 3, block 3, lesson 1
Lesson type	Revise/Teach
Lesson focus	**From Year 2: suffixes '-ness' and '-ful' following a consonant**
Resources needed	Supporting Resource 3.15 ('-ness' and '-ful')
Teaching activity	Choose a few words from the resource that end in a consonant and display on the board. Add the correct suffix. What do pupils notice about the spelling and meaning? Which other words in the list would work in the same way? What if they end in a 'y' or an 'e'? Pupils make notes in their spelling journal to help remember these words.

Lesson	Year 3, block 3, lesson 2
Lesson type	Practise/Apply
Lesson focus	**From Year 2: suffixes '-ness' and '-ful' following a consonant**
Resources needed	Supporting Resource 3.15 ('-ness' and '-ful' word cards)
Teaching activity	Pupils look at their journals and remind each other how to add '-ful' and '-ness' to words. They try out one of each and write it in their journals. Make word cards from the resource and place the words around the classroom. Pupils use cards with '-ful' and '-ness' on. They move around and add their cards to the root words. They decide which words are correct and add them to their journals.

Lesson	Year 3, block 3, lesson 3
Lesson type	Teach
Lesson focus	**Prefixes 'sub-' and 'tele-'**
Resources needed	Supporting Resource 3.16 ('sub-' and 'tele-' word cards), spelling journals
Teaching activity	Pupils work in pairs. Give them a range of the words and prefixes on cards. They put them together to make words. They list the words in their spelling journals. Create a class list and discuss the possible meanings of each prefix. **Notes:** • 'Sub-' means 'underneath'. • 'Tele-' means 'at a distance' or 'long distance'.

Block 3 – spring first half term

Lesson	Year 3, block 3, lesson 4
Lesson type	Practise
Lesson focus	**Prefixes 'sub-' and 'tele-'**
Resources needed	Supporting Resource 3.17 ('sub-' and 'tele-' words and definitions), spelling journals
Teaching activity	Go back to the lists of words in pupils' spelling journals. Revise the meaning of each prefix. Pupils record the meanings in their journals. Read out the definitions from the resource and ask pupils to write down the correct word. You could also use the cards as a sorting game.

Lesson	Year 3, block 3, lesson 5
Lesson type	Apply
Lesson focus	**Prefixes 'sub-' and 'tele-'**
Resources needed	Supporting resource 3.16 ('sub-' and 'tele-' word cards), whiteboards
Teaching activity	Read out a word from the resource and ask pupils to write it on their whiteboards. Try to put the words into sentences for pupils. They only need to write the word. They hold them up to show you so you can check spelling.

Lesson	Year 3, block 3, lesson 6
Lesson type	Practise
Lesson focus	**From Year 2: apostrophe for contraction**
Resources needed	Spelling journals
Teaching activity	Choose a couple of contractions that pupils do not write correctly. Get pupils to Quickwrite them. Ensure that the correct handwriting style is used.

Block 3 – spring first half term

Lesson	Year 3, block 3, lesson 7
Lesson type	Learn
Lesson focus	**Strategies for learning words: words from statutory and personal lists**
Resources needed	Statutory word list for Years 3 and 4 (page 49)
Teaching activity	Choose five words from statutory list. Discuss their meanings and how pupils might remember them. Add some words from personal lists. Pupils use one of the strategies already taught to learn them: • Identifying the tricky part of the word • Pyramid words • Trace, copy, replicate • Look, say, cover, write, check • Drawing around the word to show the shape.

Lesson	Year 3, block 3, lesson 8
Lesson type	Apply
Lesson focus	**Words from statutory and personal spelling lists: pair testing**
Resources needed	Statutory word list for Years 3 and 4 (page 49)
Teaching activity	Refer to the words learnt in the last session. In pairs, pupils test each other. If some words are spelt incorrectly, discuss the strategies used and make suggestions about some that might be more appropriate. Get pupils to learn the incorrectly spelt words. They can take them home for further learning.

Lesson	Year 3, block 3, lesson 9
Lesson type	Teach
Lesson focus	**Words with the /ʃ/ sound spelt 'ch' (mostly French in origin) as well as 's', 'ss(ion/ure)'**
Resources needed	Supporting Resource 3.18 (/ʃ/ sound word cards)
Teaching activity	Hand out the words to pupils in pairs. They all contain the /ʃ/ sound. Pupils read them in pairs and then share them as a group. Display the words. Add sound buttons under each word and identify ways of spelling /ʃ/. Record these in the classroom so that pupils have access to the different graphemes for /ʃ/.

Block 3 – spring first half term

Lesson	Year 3, block 3, lesson 10
Lesson type	Practise
Lesson focus	**Strategies for learning words: words with the /ʃ/ sound spelt 'ch' (mostly French in origin) as well as 's', 'ss(ion/ure)'**
Resources needed	Supporting Resource 3.18 (/ʃ/ sound word cards)
Teaching activity	Pupils learn how to spell the words using one of strategies that they have identified as working for them.

Lesson	Year 3, block 3, lesson 11
Lesson type	Apply
Lesson focus	**Words with the /ʃ/ sound spelt 'ch' (mostly French in origin) as well as 's', 'ss(ion/ure)': dictation**
Resources needed	Spelling journals
Teaching activity	Dictate the following sentences for pupils to write in their journals: *The chef used sugar in the special cake.* *The brochure was for a shop in the town.* Check them together and add tricky ones to pupils' personal spelling lists.

Lesson	Year 3, block 3, lesson 12
Lesson type	Learn
Lesson focus	**Strategies for learning words: words from statutory and personal spelling lists**
Resources needed	Statutory word list for Years 3 and 4 (page 49)
Teaching activity	Choose five words from the statutory list. Discuss their meanings and how pupils might remember them. Add some words from personal lists. Pupils use one of the strategies already taught to learn them: • Pyramid words • Identifying tricky part of the word • Trace, copy, replicate • Look, say, cover, write, check • Drawing around the word to show the shape. Send words home for pupils for further learning.

Block 3 – spring first half term

Lesson	Year 3, block 3, lesson 13
Lesson type	Revise/Teach
Lesson focus	**Revise suffixes '-ness' and '-ful'** **Teach suffixes '-less' and '-ly'**
Resources needed	Supporting Resources 3.19 (core words) and 3.20 (suffix table)
Teaching activity	Display the word cards with the core words. Extend the table and give pupils copies to fill in. They should complete it for several core words, adding '-less' and '-ful' in the way that 'care' has been modelled (*care/careless/careful*). Now add '-ly' to the resulting words (*carefully/carelessly*). Discuss as a class which words require changes to the spelling of the core word when the suffixes are added, for example.

Lesson	Year 3, block 3, lesson 14
Lesson type	Practise
Lesson focus	**Suffixes '-less', '-ness', '-ful' and '-ly'**
Resources needed	Supporting Resource 3.21 (suffix matrix)
Teaching activity	Display the matrix chart and ask pupils to create as many words as they can with the suffixes '-ful', '-ness', '-less', and '-ly'. They record them in their journals.

Lesson	Year 3, block 3, lesson 15
Lesson type	Assess
Lesson focus	**Suffixes '-less', '-ness', '-ful' and '-ly'**
Resources needed	Spelling journals or paper for writing
Teaching activity	Give the class a spelling test using the suffixes practised in the last session but on unlearnt words, for example: *loudly, gladly, badly, cheerful, handful, dutiful, restless, endless, tasteless*

Block 4 – spring 2nd half term

Lesson	Year 3, block 4, lessons 1–3
Lesson type	Practise/Revise
Lesson focus	**Strategies at the point of writing: Have a go** **Elements from the previous half term that require practice**
Resources needed	Statutory word list for Years 3 and 4 (page 49)
Teaching activity	Spend at least one session focusing on statutory words learnt so far this year. Test pupils and give them an opportunity to go back and learn those not spelt correctly. Spend one session remodelling and reinforcing Have a go routines and strategies. Model using GPC charts, words in the environment, segmentation and counting syllables as ways for having a go at unknown spellings.

Lesson	Year 3, block 4, lesson 4
Lesson type	Teach
Lesson focus	**Prefixes 'super-' and 'auto-'**
Resources needed	Supporting Resource 3.22 ('super-' and 'auto-' word cards)
Teaching activity	Display the words from the resource. Pupils write them down, making sure they know the meanings.

Lesson	Year 3, block 4, lesson 5
Lesson type	Practise
Lesson focus	**Prefixes 'super-' and 'auto-'**
Resources needed	Supporting resource 3.22 ('super-' and 'auto-' word cards)
Teaching activity	Practise handwriting for 'auto-' and 'super-' words. Remind pupils of the idea of drawing around the words or arranging them to help remember the spelling. Do this for a small selection of the 'auto-' and 'super-' words that pupils want to remember.

Lesson	Year 3, block 4, lesson 6
Lesson type	Apply
Lesson focus	**Prefixes 'super-' and 'auto-'**
Resources needed	Supporting Resource 3.22 ('super-' and 'auto-' word cards), individual whiteboards
Teaching activity	Dictate some 'super-' and 'auto-' words in the context of sentences. Pupils write down each word on their whiteboards and show them to check the spellings.

Block 4 – spring 2nd half term

Lesson	Year 3, block 4, lesson 7
Lesson type	Learn
Lesson focus	**Strategies for learning words: words from statutory and personal spelling lists**
Resources needed	Statutory word list for years 3 and 4 (page 49)
Teaching activity	Choose five words from the statutory list. Discuss their meanings and how pupils might remember them. Add some words from personal lists. Use one of the strategies already taught to learn them: • Pyramid words • Identifying tricky part of the word • Trace, copy, replicate • Look, say, cover, write, check • Drawing around the word to show the shape • Drawing a mnemonic around a word Send words home with pupils for further learning.

Lesson	Year 3, block 4, lesson 8
Lesson type	Assess
Lesson focus	**Words from the statutory and personal spelling lists: pair testing**
Resources needed	Statutory word list for Years 3 and 4 (page 49)
Teaching activity	Pupils work in pairs to test each other on their spellings. Tell pupils to identify words not spelt correctly and work on these using strategies that they know work well for them.

Lesson	Year 3, block 4, lesson 9
Lesson type	Teach
Lesson focus	**Strategies at the point of writing: homophones**
Resources needed	Supporting Resource 3.23 (homophones word cards), spelling journals
Teaching activity	Choose homophones that pupils are spelling incorrectly in their work, as well as those on the resource. Display the words and discuss as a class ways to make the spellings more memorable, for example, *there is an ear in* hear. As a class, get pupils to create sentences around each homophone orally. They record them in their journals.

Block 4 – spring 2nd half term

Lesson	Year 3, block 4, lesson 10
Lesson type	Practise
Lesson focus	**Strategies at the point of writing: homophones**
Resources needed	Individual whiteboards
Teaching activity	Read out the following sentences. Pupils write down the correct homophone on their whiteboards and hold them up to show spelling. *It is nice to meet you.* *I hear that you are walking home.* *Do you like meat and vegetables?* *It is not fair that I can't have all the chocolate.* *If your laces get in a knot, you have to undo them carefully.*

Lesson	Year 3, block 4, lesson 11
Lesson type	Apply
Lesson focus	**Homophones**
Resources needed	Individual whiteboards
Teaching activity	Invite two pupils to come up to the board. Show them a pair of homophones, so that the other pupils can't see. Each child draws a picture to represent his or her word on the board. When the others know what the word is, they write it on their whiteboards. They show them so you can check spelling.

Lesson	Year 3, block 4, lesson 12
Lesson type	Revise
Lesson focus	**Proofreading**
Resources needed	Supporting Resource 3.24 (incorrect sentences), spelling journals
Teaching activity	Display the misspelled sentences on the board. Pupils should be able to recognise the errors as the spellings have all been taught. Ask pupils to work through them, writing corrections in their journals. Check through as a class.

Lesson	Year 3, block 4, lesson 13
Lesson type	Apply
Lesson focus	**Proofreading**
Resources needed	Spelling journals
Teaching activity	Ahead of this session, mark pupils' writing from other lessons, putting a star next to sentences where spelling needs to be checked. Pupils make alterations in a different coloured pen or pencil.

Block 4 – spring 2nd half term

Lesson	Year 3, block 4, lesson 14
Lesson type	Learn
Lesson focus	**Strategies for learning words: words from statutory and personal spelling lists**
Resources needed	Statutory word list for Years 3 and 4 (page 49)
Teaching activity	Choose five words from the statutory list. Discuss their meanings and how pupils might remember them. Add some words from personal lists. Use one of the strategies already taught to learn them: • Pyramid words • Identifying tricky part of the word • Trace, copy, replicate • Look, say, cover, write, check • Drawing around the word to show the shape • Drawing a mnenomic around a word Send words home for pupils for further learning.

Lesson	Year 3, block 4, lesson 15
Lesson type	Teach/Apply
Lesson focus	**Words with the /k/ sound spelt 'ch' (Greek in origin)**
Resources needed	Supporting Resource 3.25 (/k/ spelt 'ch' pictures and words), spelling journals
Teaching activity	Show the images with the words underneath. Ask pupils to look at the spellings carefully and write out the words in their spelling journals. They should notice the part that is tricky. Remove the words from the display and ask pupils to write the words themselves on a new page.

No Nonsense Spelling

Year 3 Term 3 overview

Block 5 – summer first half term

Week 1	Lesson 1 Revise **Previously taught suffixes ('-ed', '-ing', '-s', '-es', '-ness', '-ful', '-less' and '-ly')**	Lesson 2 Practise **Previously taught suffixes ('-ed', '-ing', '-s', '-es', '-ness', '-ful', '-less' and '-ly')**	Lesson 3 Apply **Previously taught suffixes: dictation**
Week 2	Lesson 4 Teach **Suffix '-ly' with root words ending in 'le' and 'ic'**	Lesson 5 Practise **Suffix '-ly'**	Lesson 6 Apply **Suffix '-ly'**
Week 3	Lesson 7 Revise **From Year 2: apostrophe for contraction**	Lesson 8 Learn **Strategies for learning words: words from statutory and personal spelling lists**	Lesson 9 Assess **Words from statutory and personal spelling lists**
Week 4	Lesson 10 Teach **Rare GPCs (/ɪ/ sound)**	Lesson 11 Practise **Rare GPCs (/ɪ/ sound)**	
Week 5	Lesson 12 Apply **Rare GPCs (/ɪ/ sound)**	Lesson 13 Learn **Strategies for learning words: words from statutory and personal spelling lists**	Lesson 14 Practise **Strategies for learning words: words from statutory and personal spelling lists**
Week 6	Lesson 15 Apply/Assess **Words from statutory and personal spelling lists**	Lesson 16 Revise **From Years 1 and 2: vowel digraphs**	

Block 6 – summer second half term

Week 1	Lesson 1 Revise **Strategies at the point of writing: Have a go** **Spellings learnt in the last half term**	Lesson 2 Revise **Spellings learnt in the last half term**	Lesson 3 Revise **Spellings learnt in the last half term**
Week 2	Lesson 4 Teach **The /ʌ/ sound spelt 'ou'**	Lesson 5 Practise **The /ʌ/ sound spelt 'ou'**	
Week 3	Lesson 6 Apply **The /ʌ/ sound spelt 'ou': dictation**	Lesson 7 Learn **Strategies for learning words: words from statutory and personal spelling lists**	Lesson 8 Assess **Words from statutory and personal spelling lists: pair testing**
Week 4	Lesson 9 Teach **Homophones (including heel/heal/he'll, plain/plane, groan/grown and rain/rein/reign)**	Lesson 10 Practise **Homophones (including heel/heal/he'll, plain/plane, groan/grown and rain/rein/reign)**	
Week 5	Lesson 11 Apply **Homophones (including heel/heal/he'll, plain/plane, groan/grown and rain/rein/reign)**	Lesson 12 Teach **Proofreading**	Lesson 13 Learn **Strategies for learning words: words from statutory and personal spelling lists**
Week 6	Lesson 14 Apply **Words from statutory and personal spelling lists**	Lesson 15 Revise **Aspects from this half term**	

Block 5 – summer first half term

Lesson	Year 3, block 5, lesson 1
Lesson type	Revise
Lesson focus	**Previously taught suffixes ('-ed', '-ing', '-s', '-es', '-ness', '-ful', '-less' and '-ly')**
Resources needed	Spelling journals
Teaching activity	Pupils share their understanding of a suffix and list those that they know. They practise handwriting these suffixes. Where are the issues with spelling these? Issues are likely to be in cases where they have to double the consonant or remove the 'e' from the root word. Use a range of words and explore ways pupils can remember the tricky one. Try out on a few words. **Notes** • A short vowel means you must double the consonant. • If the root word ends in '-e' this is dropped when adding a suffix beginning with a vowel letter (the exception in 'being').

Lesson	Year 3, block 5, lesson 2
Lesson type	Practise
Lesson focus	**Previously taught suffixes ('-ed', '-ing', '-s', '-es', '-ness', '-ful', '-less' and '-ly')**
Resources needed	Supporting Resource 3.26 (root words for suffixes)
Teaching activity	Use a longer list of words from the supporting resource. Pupils write them in their spelling journals, adding suffixes to them and thinking about any spelling changes – for example, *hope, hoping, hopes, hoped, hopeful.* They check with a partner. Collect more examples that pupils have seen in their reading and add to the Working wall.

Lesson	Year 3, block 5, lesson 3
Lesson type	Apply
Lesson focus	**Previously taught suffixes: dictation**
Resources needed	Spelling journals
Teaching activity	Get pupils to Quickwrite the words and suffixes that they find tricky. Dictate the following sentences and check spellings afterwards. *He hops and skips and smiles on his way to school.* *I am hoping that when Jo hopped she didn't hurt her knee.* *We are phoning the school and stopping the sharing of lollies.*

No Nonsense Spelling

No Nonsense Spelling Programme

Block 5 – summer first half term

Lesson	Year 3, block 5, lesson 4
Lesson type	Teach
Lesson focus	**Suffix '-ly' with root words ending in 'le' and 'ic'**
Resources needed	Supporting Resource 3.27 ('-ly' matrix)
Teaching activity	Use the matrix, concentrating on the words ending in '-le' and '-ic'. As a class, read the words and add '-ly' to each. Discuss how they might be written down. This will be practised in the next lesson.

Lesson	Year 3, block 5, lesson 5
Lesson type	Practise
Lesson focus	**Suffix '-ly'**
Resources needed	Supporting Resource 3.27 ('-ly' matrix)
Teaching activity	Go back to the list used in the previous session and make up some conventions for adding '-ly'. Add a few more words to the chart: *friend, kind, week, lone, near, free*. Pupils use the conventions they have made and write down all the words, adding '-ly' to them. Check them. Pupils can take these words home to learn. **Notes**: • The suffix '-ly' starts with a consonant letter, so is added straight on to most root words. • If the root word ends in consonant letter 'y', the 'y' is changed to 'i', but only if the word is more than one syllable. • If the root words ends in 'le', the 'le' is changed to 'ly'. • If the root word ends with 'ic', then '-ally' is added rather than just '-ly' (exception: *publicly*).

Lesson	Year 3, block 5, lesson 6
Lesson type	Apply
Lesson focus	**Suffix '-ly'**
Resources needed	Supporting Resource 3.27 ('-ly' matrix)
Teaching activity	Reflect as a class on what you have learnt about adding '-ly'. Ask pupils to write notes in their journals. Using a range of the '-ly' words, get pupils to generate and write sentences with the words included.

Block 5 – summer first half term

Lesson	Year 3, block 5, lesson 7
Lesson type	Revise
Lesson focus	**From Year 2: apostrophe for contraction**
Resources needed	Supporting Resource 3.28 (full words for contraction)
Teaching activity	Pupils share why an apostrophe is used for a contraction. Display the full words from the resource. Add any that you know pupils do not write correctly. Pupils write down the contractions in their journals. Ask pupils to look through their own writing for examples of apostrophes for contraction. They should correct them if not used correctly.

Lesson	Year 3, block 5, lesson 8
Lesson type	Learn
Lesson focus	**Strategies for learning words: words from statutory and personal spelling lists**
Resources needed	Statutory word list for Years 3 and 4 (page 49)
Teaching activity	Choose five words from the statutory list. Discuss their meanings and how pupils might remember them. Add some words from personal lists. Use one of the strategies already taught to learn them: - Pyramid words - Identifying tricky part of the word - Trace, copy, replicate - Look, say, cover, write, check - Drawing around the word to show the shape - Drawing a mnemonic around a word Send words home for pupils for further learning.

Lesson	Year 3, block 5, lesson 9
Lesson type	Assess
Lesson focus	**Words from statutory and personal spelling lists**
Resources needed	Statutory and personal spelling lists
Teaching activity	Get pupils to test each other on their words in pairs. Stick their spelling tests into their journals. Pupils can take this home to share with their parents how well they did. Those that need more work on this may need an extra session here.

Block 5 – summer first half term

Lesson	Year 3, block 5, lesson 10
Lesson type	Teach
Lesson focus	**Rare GPCs (/ɪ/ sound)**
Resources needed	Supporting Resource 3.29 (rare GPCs for /ɪ/ pictures)
Teaching activity	Show pupils a range of images from the resource and ask them to say what they can see. They will have seen some in the previous lesson on 'y' making /ɪ/. Get pupils to sound out the words and write them down in their spelling journals. What do pupils notice? They should see that there are some more unusual ways of making the /ɪ/ sound. (*Answers: gym, cygnet, myth, pretty, women, pyramid, mystery, Egypt, build*) Any words that are not learnt should be carried over to an extra session the next day.

Lesson	Year 3, block 5, lesson 11
Lesson type	Practise
Lesson focus	**Rare GPCs (/ɪ/ sound)**
Resources needed	List of words made in the last lesson
Teaching activity	Using the words they wrote down in the last lesson, ask pupils to write them into sentences. Ask them to read out their sentences for others to write down. Check spellings of words.

Lesson	Year 3, block 5, lesson 12
Lesson type	Apply
Lesson focus	**Rare GPCs (/ɪ/ sound)**
Resources needed	Words and sentences from lessons 10 and 11
Teaching activity	Ask pupils to Quickwrite the words from lesson 10 for 30 seconds each. In pairs, pupils read their sentences from the previous lesson to a partner who writes them. Check they have spelt the words correctly.

Block 5 – summer first half term

Lesson	Year 3, block 5, lesson 13
Lesson type	Learn
Lesson focus	**Strategies for learning words: words from statutory and personal spelling lists**
Resources needed	Statutory word list for Years 3 and 4 (page 49)
Teaching activity	Choose five words from the statutory list and some words from individual lists. Pupils have six ways that they know how to learn words: • Pyramid words • Identifying tricky part of the word • Trace, copy, replicate • Look, say, cover, write, check • Drawing around the word to show the shape • Drawing a mnemonic around a word Pupils learn the new words.

Lesson	Year 3, block 5, lesson 14
Lesson type	Practise
Lesson focus	**Strategies for learning words: words from statutory and personal spelling lists**
Resources needed	Statutory word list for Years 3 and 4 (page 49)
Teaching activity	Practise handwriting using words from the statutory list. Write each word 10 times. Take words home to practise.

Lesson	Year 3, block 5, lesson 15
Lesson type	Apply/Assess
Lesson focus	**Words from statutory and personal spelling lists**
Resources needed	Statutory word list for Years 3 and 4 (page 49)
Teaching activity	In pairs, pupils test each other on the words they have been learning. They identify those words not spelt correctly and learn them using different strategies. You may need to provide an extra session here for learning and peer testing.

Block 5 – summer first half term

Lesson	Year 3, block 5, lesson 16
Lesson type	Revise
Lesson focus	**From Years 1 and 2: vowel digraphs**
Resources needed	Supporting Resource 3.30 (example grapheme family table)
Teaching activity	Choose three or four vowel digraphs that pupils are not secure with when writing – these may be included in topic words or from other areas of the curriculum. Follow the example table on the Supporting Resource to create similar tables for the phonemes you want to concentrate on. Dictate some words that have each phoneme in. Pupils write the words under each spelling. The completed grapheme family tables can be kept out for pupils to refer to when using their Have a go sheets and writing words that have the phonemes in.

Block 6 – summer 2nd half term

Lesson	Year 3, block 6, lessons 1–3
Lesson type	Revise
Lesson focus	**Strategies at the point of writing: Have a go** **Spellings learnt in the last half term**
Resources needed	Statutory word list for Years 3 and 4 (page 49)
Teaching activity	These are three sessions to revise and review last half term. Choose elements to focus on based on pupils' writing and their spelling work. Spend at least one session testing pupils on the statutory spelling list words that they have learnt so far over the year. Revise those not spelt correctly. Spend at least one session revising the use of Have a go routines and strategies. Remodel the approach including using GPC charts, words in the environment and other taught strategies. Continue to model and apply in all writing across the curriculum.

Lesson	Year 3, block 6, lesson 4
Lesson type	Teach
Lesson focus	**The /ʌ/ sound spelt 'ou'**
Resources needed	Supporting Resource 3.31 ('ou' word cards)
Teaching activity	Share the words from the resource and identify the sound that the 'ou' makes in each word. Draw attention to the spelling of the /f/ phoneme at the end of 'rough'. This is a very unusual example. Ask pupils to sound out each word and write it down. They then draw a box around the 'ou' and 'take a picture of it', committing it to memory.

Lesson	Year 3, block 6, lesson 5
Lesson type	Practise
Lesson focus	**The /ʌ/ sound spelt 'ou'**
Resources needed	Supporting Resource 3.31 ('ou' word cards)
Teaching activity	Give pupils copies of the words to share between two. In pairs, pupils take it in turns to read out an 'ou' word. Their partner writes the word down. They check the spelling on the card and identify those that need further work. Send these words home for further learning.

Block 6 – summer 2nd half term

Lesson	Year 3, block 6, lesson 6
Lesson type	Apply
Lesson focus	The /ʌ/ sound spelt 'ou': dictation
Resources needed	Spelling journals
Teaching activity	Dictate the following sentences for pupils to write: *You will be in trouble if you touch the young plant.* *The countryside is rough to walk on.* Check the spellings.

Lesson	Year 3, block 6, lesson 7
Lesson type	Learn
Lesson focus	**Strategies for learning words: words from statutory and personal spelling lists**
Resources needed	Statutory word list for Years 3 and 4 (page 49)
Teaching activity	Choose five words from statutory list and some words from individual lists. Pupils have six ways that they know how to learn words: • Pyramid words • Identifying tricky part of the word • Trace, copy, replicate • Look, say, cover, write, check • Drawing around the word to show the shape • Drawing a mnemonic around a word Pupils learn new words Take words home to practise further. If pupils need an extra session, add one in here.

Lesson	Year 3, block 6, lesson 8
Lesson type	Assess
Lesson focus	**Words from statutory and personal spelling lists: pair testing**
Resources needed	Statutory word list for Years 3 and 4 (page 49)
Teaching activity	Get pupils to test each other's spellings in pairs. Take feedback on how well everyone has done. Which words are still tricky? Make sure that any words that were spelt incorrectly are added to a list of words to learn next time.

Block 6 – summer 2nd half term

Lesson	Year 3, block 6, lesson 9
Lesson type	Teach
Lesson focus	**Homophones (including *heel/heal/he'll*, *plain/plane*, *groan/grown* and *rain/rein/reign*)**
Resources needed	Supporting Resource 3.32
Teaching activity	Introduce the homophones and their meanings. Use those from pupils' writing but also include those from the resource. Challenge pupils to try to create sentences that contain both or all of the words – for example, *He'll find that his heel won't heal*. Write their sentences down on strips of card to use in the next lesson.

Lesson	Year 3, block 6, lesson 10
Lesson type	Practise
Lesson focus	**Homophones (including *heel/heal/he'll*, *plain/plane*, *groan/grown* and *rain/rein/reign*)**
Resources needed	Sentence cards made in lesson 9
Teaching activity	Pupils choose a strip of card with a sentence on. They read it out to two friends who write it down. They check spellings and then another person from the group chooses a sentence to read out.

Lesson	Year 3, block 6, lesson 11
Lesson type	Apply
Lesson focus	**Homophones (including *heel/heal/he'll*, *plain/plane*, *groan/grown* and *rain/rein/reign*)**
Resources needed	Sentence cards made in lesson 9
Teaching activity	Play a relay race to review homophones. Divide your class into six groups and have one person from each group come to the front of the line where a large piece of paper is displayed for their team. Read a sentence that uses one of a pair of homophones. If they write the word correctly their team gains a point. The winning team has the most points.

Block 6 – summer 2nd half term

Lesson	Year 3, block 6, lesson 12
Lesson type	Teach
Lesson focus	**Proofreading**
Resources needed	A range of sentences from pupils' own work, spelling journals
Teaching activity	Use a range of sentences with spelling errors. The errors should be in aspects that have been taught throughout the year. As a class, pupils identify the errors and correct them in their journals.

Lesson	Year 3, block 6, lesson 13
Lesson type	Learn
Lesson focus	**Strategies for learning words: words from statutory and personal spelling lists**
Resources needed	Statutory word list for Years 3 and 4 (page 49)
Teaching activity	Choose five words from the statutory list and some words from individual lists. Pupils have at least six ways that they know to help them learn words: • Pyramid words • Identifying the tricky part of the word • Trace, copy, replicate • Look, say, cover, write, check • Drawing around the word to show the shape • Drawing a mnemonic around a word Pupils learn the new words. They can take them home to practise further. If pupils need an extra session, add one in here.

Lesson	Year 3, block 6, lesson 14
Lesson type	Apply
Lesson focus	**Words from statutory and personal spelling lists**
Resources needed	Statutory word list for Years 3 and 4 (page 49)
Teaching activity	In pairs, pupils test each other on their spellings. Take feedback on how well everyone has done. Which words are still tricky? Focus on these words in any extra sessions.

Lesson	Year 3, block 6, lesson 15
Lesson type	Revise
Lesson focus	**Aspects from this half term**
Resources needed	Various
Teaching activity	Revise key aspects from this half term as needed by pupils.

Statutory word list for Years 3 and 4

accident(ally)	famous	peculiar
actual(ly)	favourite	perhaps
address	February	popular
answer	forward(s)	position
appear	fruit	possess(ion)
arrive	grammar	possible
believe	group	potatoes
bicycle	guard	pressure
breath	guide	probably
breathe	heard (h)	promise
build	heart	quarter
busy/business	height	question
calendar	history	recent
caught	imagine	regular
centre	important	reign (h)
century	increase	remember
certain	interest	sentence
circle	island	separate
complete	knowledge	special
consider	learn	straight
continue	length	strange
decide	library	strength
describe	material	suppose
different (Phase 5)	medicine	surprise
difficult	mention	therefore
disappear	minute	though/although
early	natural	thought (Phase 5)
earth	naughty	through (Phase 5) (h)
eight (h)/eighth	notice	various
enough	occasion(ally)	weight (h)
exercise	often	woman/women
experience	opposite	
experiment	ordinary	
extreme	particular	

Year 3 Supporting Resources

Error Analysis template 3.1

Name _____   Class _____   Date _____

Common exception words	GPC (includes rare GPCs and vowel digraphs)	Homophones	Prefixes and suffixes	Word endings	Other

Have a go template 3.2

My column	Teacher's column	My column	Teacher's column

No Nonsense Spelling

GPC chart 3.3

These charts show the phonemes of English represented by the International Phonetic Alphabet together with their common grapheme representations. All Phase 5 GPCs are included together with other less common grapheme choices needed in Year 2 and above. The correspondences in the table are based on Received Pronunciation and could be significantly different in other accents. One example word is provided for each phoneme to support teachers unfamiliar with IPA. Other examples can be found in Appendix 1 of the National Curriculum.

Consonant GPCs

/b/ bat	/d/ dog	/ð/ mother	/dʒ/ jug	/f/ fish	/g/ goat	/h/ hand	/j/ yawn	/k/ cat	/l/ and /əl/ lamp, bottle	/m/ mouse	/n/ nail
b bb	d dd	th	j g ge dge	f ff ph	g gg gu gue	h	y	c k ck ch q que	l ll le el al il	m mm mb	n nn kn gn pn mn

/ŋ/ wing	/θ/ thumb	/p/ pin	/r/ rain	/s/ sun	/ʃ/ ship	/t/ tap	/tʃ/ chick	/v/ van	/w/ watch	/z/ zip
ng n(k)	th	p	r rr wr	s ss se sc c ce	sh ch ti ci ss(ion, ure) s (ion, ure	t tt	ch tch t	v ve	w wh u	z zz ze s se x

Note: The letter **x** in English frequently represents 2 adjacent consonant phonemes /k/ and /s/, for example in the word **box**.

Vowel GPCs

/ɑː/ arm	/ɒ/ hot	/æ/ cat	/aɪ/ pie	/aʊ/ cow	/ɛ/ hen	/eɪ/ day	/ɛə/ pair	/əʊ/ boat	/ɪ/ pin
ar a	o a	a	igh i-e ie i y	ow ou	e ea	ai ay a-e a aigh ei eigh ey	air are ear	ow oa oe o-e o	i y e

/ɪə/ cheer	/iː/ bean	/ɔː/ fork	/ɔɪ/ boy	/ʊ/ book	/ʊə/ cure	/uː/ blue	/ʌ/ cup	/ɜː/ girl
ear eer ere	ea ee e-e ie y ey e ei eo	or oor ore aw au our a al ar	oy oi	oo u oul	ure our	oo u-e ue ew ui ou ough	u o	er ir ur or ear

Note: The symbol /ə/, known as "schwa" represents the unstressed phoneme in many English words. It can be spelt in many different ways, for example **er** as in farm**er**.

No Nonsense Spelling

Year 3 – Block 1 – Lesson 1 3.4

	walk	
	run	
	skip	
	chat	
	sing	s
	search	es
	hope	ed
	wave	ing
	reach	er
	smile	
	like	
	bake	
	plan	
	float	
	clap	
	run	

Year 3 – Block 1 – Lesson 2 3.5

Today

Sophie looks for a book.

Ahmed counts to ten.

Alice wants to cook.

George searches for a pen.

Archie hops in the playground.

Mia skips around.

Year 3 – Block 1 – Lesson 3   3.6

happy	like
lucky	please
seen	agree
usual	own
do	appear
tie	obey
zip	honest
dress	trust
well	allow
fold	order

Year 3 – Block 1 – Lesson 5   3.7

does not	I have	she is/has
can not	I had	it is/has
will not	I would	he is/has
do not	I am	there is/has
is not	I will	

No Nonsense Spelling

Year 3 – Block 1 – Lessons 8, 9 and 12 3.8

The stars identify homophones. Choose some words from these lists.

ate* grade made* trade bake brake* shake* stake* male* sale* vale* game flame frame mane* plane* tape grape scrape chase gate* grate* plate skate paste taste waste* brave	aid aim paid fail mail* sail* tail* snail claim main* pain* chain plain* stain strain vain* wait* gait* paint faint waist* again afraid entail explain complain contain detail obtain maintain remain	reins* vein* veil* reign* neigh weigh* sleigh* eight* freight weight*	acorn baby data alien apron agent basic basin	play way say day Monday Tuesday Wednesday Thursday Friday Saturday Sunday crayfish playground	straight	grey prey* they obey convey survey

Year 3 – Block 1 – Lesson 9   3.9

No Nonsense Spelling

Year 3 – Block 1 – Lesson 13 3.10

The playground is over _____.
It was _____ dog that bit the postman.
_____ sleeping over at a friend's house tonight.
The _____ was shining brightly.
My _____ is in the army.
I have _____ sweets and four bags of crisps.
I _____ my pizza really quickly.
Why won't you _____ your coat?
_____ is your coat?
The glass will _____ if you throw the ball.
The bike's _____ didn't work.

Year 3 – Block 1 – Lesson 14 3.11

Year 3 – Block 2 – Lesson 3   3.12

	nice late ripe rude	er
	brave hike ride write	est

bad play hope care happy sad colour harm	ful less	ly

	copy worry happy cry reply funny	er est ed ing

fair sad kind tidy lovely silly nasty happy willing fit foolish	ness	enjoy employ docu oint state move	ment

Year 3 – Block 2 – Lesson 4 3.13

appear	try	remember
build	take	write
play	behave	hear
do	apply	calculate
turn	take	read

Year 3 – Block 2 – Lessons 9 and 10 3.14

Year 3 – Block 3 – Lessons 1 and 2   3.15

ful	ness	wish	fair
ful	ness	hope	kind
ful	ness	forget	lovely
ful	ness	pity	nasty
ful	ness	hate	fit
ful	ness	beauty	foolish
ful	ness	pain	tidy
ful	ness	success	happy

Year 3 – Block 3 – Lesson 3   3.16

tele	tele	tele	tele
sub	sub	sub	sub
phone	graph	scope	vision
photo	marine	way	terranean
merge	ordinate		soil

Year 3 – Block 3 – Lesson 4 3.17

look through this to see things from far away	telescope
the thing you watch your favourite programmes on	television
a clause that does not make sense on its own	subordinate
an invention that sent messages quickly over long distances	telegraph
use this to speak to people far away	telephone
an underground tunnel or passage enabling pedestrians to cross a road or railway	subway
an underwater ship	submarine
fill or cover completely, usually with water	submerge

Year 3 – Block 3 – Lessons 9 and 10 3.18

chef	shop	sure	mission
special	brochure	sugar	

No Nonsense Spelling

Year 3 – Block 3 – Lesson 13 3.19

care	thank	slow	rough
joy	mercy	quick	careful
job	thought	sudden	angry
fear	pain	sad	happy

Year 3 – Block 3 – Lesson 13 3.20

core word	less	ful	ly
care	careless	careful	carelessly carefully
thought			

Year 3 – Block 3 – Lesson 14 3.21

| care hope harm use help thank | less ful | ness ly |

Year 3 – Block 4 – Lessons 4–6 3.22

automatic	autopilot	autobiography
autograph	autonomy	autofocus
superman	superior	supernatural
superstar	superior	superficial

Year 3 – Block 4 – Lesson 9 3.23

meet	meat
hear	here
knot	not

Year 3 – Block 4 – Lesson 12 3.24

That girl is really beautyful.

I cannt come out today.

The broshure from the hotel looks grate.

Dont brake that window!

There sleeping over at my friend's house tonight.

You have made to many mistakes.

No Nonsense Spelling

Year 3 – Block 4 – Lesson 15 3.25

ache	anchor
Christmas	school
choir	echo

Year 3 – Block 5 – Lesson 2   3.26

hope	hop
care	chat
share	clap
like	plan
smile	rub
phone	stop
use	hug
bake	slip

Year 3 – Block 5 – Lessons 4–6   3.27

quick nice late close happy funny lucky gentle simple humble basic frantic dramatic	ly

Year 3 – Block 5 – Lesson 7 3.28

I will	is not	has not
I am	he will	will not
do not	cannot	I had
I would	I have	are not
had not	have not	could not
you are	they are	you will
he will	you have	

No Nonsense Spelling

No Nonsense Spelling Programme

Year 3 – Block 5 – Lesson 10   3.29

67

Year 3 – Block 5 – Lesson 16 3.30

\	\	The 'ee' sound family	\	\	\
ee	ea	e-e	ie	y	ey

Year 3 – Block 6 – Lessons 4 and 5 3.31

young	double	touch
trouble	country	rough

Year 3 – Block 6 – Lesson 9 3.32

heel	heal	he'll
rain	rein	reign
plain		plane
groan		grown

Notes

Notes

Notes

Notes